W9-ARA-198

Date: 12/23/15

J 940.4 LAN
Lanser, Amanda.
World War I by the numbers /

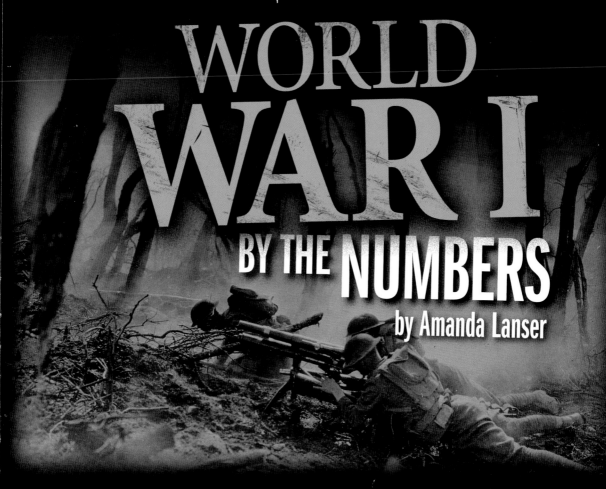

WORLD WAR I

BY THE NUMBERS

by Amanda Lanser

Consultant:

Jason Myers, PhD

Modern European History

Loyola University

Chicago, Illinois

CAPSTONE PRESS

a capstone imprint

Edge Books are published by Capstone Press,
1710 Roe Crest Drive, North Mankato, Minnesota 56003
www.capstonepub.com

Library of Congress Cataloging-in-Publication Data
Lanser, Amanda.
  World War I by the numbers / by Amanda Lanser.
     pages cm.—(Edge books. America at war by the numbers.)
  Summary: "Describes aspects of World War I using numbers, stats, and
infographics"—Provided by publisher.
  Includes bibliographical references and index.
  ISBN 978-1-4914-4296-8 (library binding)
  ISBN 978-1-4914-4332-3 (ebook pdf)
  1. World War, 1914–1918—Juvenile literature. I. Title.
  D522.7.L36 2016
  940.4—dc23   2015000536

Editorial Credits

Arnold Ringstad, editor
Craig Hinton, designer
Jake Nordby, production specialist

Photo Credits

Alamy: PF-(wararchive), 21 (bottom), Pictorial Press Ltd, 22–23, The Print Collector, 19; AP Images: 3 (left), 4, 21 (top), Bettmann/
Corbis, cover (background), cover (foreground), 1; Bibliothèque nationale de France, 14–15; Corbis: Adoc-Photos, 3 (right), 14,
Hulton-Deutsch Collection, 15, Major Tracy Evarts, 28–29; Getty Images: Archive Photos, 2, 20, DEA Picture Library/De Agostini,
16–17, Ed Vebell, 8–9 (foreground), General Photographic Agency, 24, Lt. J. W. Brooke/IWM, 10–11, Popperfoto, 17, Robert Hunt
Library/Windmill Books/UIG, 18; Library of Congress: 7, 8 (gas mask), 8–9 (background), 13 (top), 18–19, 24–25, 26, Pach Brothers,
29 (bottom); Red Line Editorial, 5, 6; Shutterstock Images: TFoxFoto, 4 (explosion), Willequet Manuel, 8–9 (background), Sociologas,
12 (metal plate); Thinkstock/Dorling Kindersley, 11; U.K. National Media Museum, 13 (bottom); U.S. Army, 12 (bottom), 26–27; U.S.
National Archives and Records Administration, 12 (top)

Design Element

Red Line Editorial (infographics); Shutterstock Images: Ken Schulze (smoke)

Printed in the United States of America in North Mankato, Minnesota.
042015   008823CGF15

Table of **Contents**

The War to End War

World War I was the most devastating war the world had seen up to that point. Some people even called it "the war to end war." It is known for machine guns, muddy trenches, rumbling tanks, and airplanes fighting in the skies over Europe. This is World War I—by the numbers.

U.S. M1917 tank

950 U.S. M1917 tanks produced by 1918

2,600 British tanks built by the summer of 1918

20 German tanks produced by 1918

Assassination of the Archduke

The **assassination** of Austro-Hungarian Archduke Franz Ferdinand and his wife, Sophie, triggered the start of World War I. Austria-Hungary had added a **province** called Bosnia to its empire in 1908. This angered people from an ethnic group called the Serbs, many of whom lived in Bosnia. They wanted the province to become part of the country of Serbia instead. Several young Serbs plotted the death of the Austro-Hungarian archduke.

June 28, 1914 date of the assassination of Archduke Franz Ferdinand

7 Bosnian Serbs who plotted to kill the archduke

1 assassin, Gavrilo Princip, who fired a pistol at the archduke's car between Appel Quay and Franz Joseph Street

Franz Joseph Street

4 assassins present when one of them threw a bomb at the archduke's car at the intersection of Appel Quay and Cumburja Bridge

0 people killed in the failed bomb assassination attempt

2 people Princip killed with his pistol—the archduke and his wife

Appel Quay

Cumburja Bridge

30 days between the archduke's assassination and the start of World War I

assassination—a murder of a government official or other leader
province—a division of a country, similar to a state

Declaring War

After wars in the 1860s and 1870s, the major nations of Europe entered a fragile period of peace. France, the United Kingdom, and Russia formed a loose **alliance**, while Germany and Austria-Hungary did the same. The two sides fought against each other in World War I.

Europe in 1916

Allied Powers
Central Powers
Neutral

Norway

Denmark

Netherlands

United Kingdom

Belgium

Luxemburg

Germany

Russia

France

Switzerland

Italy

Austria-Hungary

Romania

Montenegro

Serbia

Bulgaria

Greece

Albania

Ottoman Empire

Portugal

Spain

4
number of major Central Powers (Germany, Austria-Hungary, Ottoman Empire, and Bulgaria)

4
number of major Allied Powers (the United Kingdom, France, Russia, and Italy)

alliance—an agreement to join together
mobilize—to make ready for war
telegram—a message transmitted over a long distance

Declarations of War
1914

July 28: Austria-Hungary declares war on Serbia.

July 31: Russia **mobilizes** troops to support Serbia.

August 1: Germany declares war on Russia.

August 3: Germany declares war on France.

August 4: Germany declares war on Belgium; the United Kingdom declares war on Germany.

August 6: Austria-Hungary declares war on Russia.

The United States Goes to War

1,959 people aboard the *Lusitania*

128 Americans lost in the sinking of the *Lusitania*

1,195 lives lost in the sinking of the *Lusitania*

January 16, 1917
the United Kingdom intercepts the telegram

The deaths of American passengers on ships sunk by German submarines helped turn American public opinion against Germany. One of these ships was the *Lusitania*, which sank on May 7, 1915.

In early 1917 the United Kingdom discovered a **telegram** from Germany to Mexico. The message said that if Mexico helped Germany win the war, Mexico could take Texas and New Mexico. Americans were outraged by the telegram, and the United States soon declared war on Germany.

April 6, 1917
the United States declares war on Germany

Outfitting an AEF Doughboy

When the United States entered World War I on April 6, 1917, the army it sent to Europe was known as the American Expeditionary Force, or AEF. But individual soldiers were known as doughboys. No one is sure where the nickname came from. Some historians think the name came from the doughy rations the soldiers ate. Others think it dates back to the Mexican-American War (1846–1848), where the soldiers' uniforms would get covered with flour-colored desert soil.

1 steel helmet

1 wool uniform

1 10-pocket cartridge belt

1 gas mask bag containing 1 gas mask

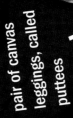

1 M1903 Springfield or M1917 Enfield rifle

4 million
soldiers and officers in the U.S. Army who had served in World War I by the end of the war

expeditionary—sent on military service in a different country

1 pair of canvas leggings, called puttees

127,500
soldiers and officers in the U.S. Army when the United States declared war on Germany

In the
Trenches

World War I has become infamous for its bloody trench warfare. Heavily defended trenches made it extremely difficult to take enemy territory. These trenches stretched for many miles through the heart of Europe during World War I. They were surrounded by millions of craters made by bombs and artillery. Land mines and barbed wire covered the area between the opposing trenches.

460 miles
distance a soldier could walk without leaving a trench along the western front between northern Belgium and France's border with Switzerland

25,000 miles
length of trenches laid by both sides, if laid end to end

800 miles
length of continuous lines of trenches along the eastern front between the Baltic Sea, which borders Germany on the north, and the Carpathian Mountains in Austria-Hungary

100 to 200 yards
average distance between Allied trenches and German ones, a space called no-man's-land

front—the area where two opposing armies meet and fight

Europe during World War I

- CENTRAL POWERS
- ALLIES
- NEUTRAL
- AREAS CONQUERED BY CENTRAL POWERS
- FRONTS

NORWAY
SWEDEN
North Sea
Baltic Sea
DENMARK
RUSSIAN EMPIRE
EASTERN FRONT
BRITAIN
NETH.
GERMANY
ATLANTIC OCEAN
WESTERN FRONT
BELGIUM
FRANCE
AUSTRIA-HUNGARY
SWITZERLAND
ROMANIA
Black Sea
PORTUGAL
SPAIN
ITALY
BULGARIA
OTTOMAN EMPIRE
GREECE
Mediterranean Sea

N W E S

3 weeks in each cycle of a British soldier's trench schedule

Week 1	Week 2	Week 3
on the front lines	in the middle support trench	in the back reserve trench

Airplanes

65,000
aircraft all sides produced during World War I

5
enemy aircraft shot down for a fighter pilot to be called an ace

80
enemy aircraft German ace "Red Baron" Manfred von Richthofen shot down

Machine Guns

1884
year the machine gun was invented

1917
year the U.S. Army begins purchasing Browning machine guns from U.S. gun manufacturers

57,000
Browning machine guns U.S. companies built by the end of the war

600
rounds per minute the average machine gun could shoot

1,000 yards
range of an average World War I machine gun

range—the longest distance at which a weapon can still hit its target

Tanks

September 15, 1916
date the British used the first tank in the Battle of Flers-Courcelette

49
British tanks involved in the Battle of Flers-Courcelette

M1917
model number of the first official tank used in the U.S. Army, first used in 1918

7.25 tons
weight of the M1917 tank

10
M1917 tanks that reached Europe by the end of 1918

Chemical Warfare

April 22, 1915
day the German Army used the first chemical weapon, chlorine gas, at Ypres, Belgium

1,000
French and Algerian soldiers killed within minutes of the gas being used

160 tons
amount of gas used that day

10 minutes
time it took the gas to drift into French trenches

124,200 tons
amount of gas produced by the end of World War I

The **Bloodiest**

Battle	Introduction
Battle of the Frontiers (August 14–September 9, 1914)	The Battle of the Frontiers is the name for several battles—the first of World War I. They were all fought along the borders between France and Germany and Germany and Belgium.
Battle of Verdun (February 21– December 18, 1916)	The Battle of Verdun was among the longest and costliest battles of the war. Between February and July 1916, the Germans launched an attack against the French town of Verdun, fighting back French troops. Between October and December, the French were able to regain the ground they lost.
Battle of the Somme (July 1–November 18, 1916)	The Battle of the Somme began as a British attack along the Somme River in northern France. It started with the British shelling the German lines. However, the shells were ineffective against the sturdy German positions. Tens of thousands of soldiers died on the first day alone. The German forces built stronger defenses, and no Allied attacks could break through them.

Battles

Length of Battle	Killed, Wounded, or Missing	Result
23 days	Germany: 300,000 France: 330,000 United Kingdom: 30,000	**German Victory**
10 months	Germany: 337,000 France: 377,231	**French Victory**
20 weeks	Germany: 465,000 France: 200,000 United Kingdom: 420,000	**No Clear Victor**

Battle on the Seas: German U-Boats

World War I introduced several new war technologies. One of the most effective was the German U-boat. Short for *Unterseeboot*, or "undersea boat," U-boats waged submarine warfare in the Atlantic Ocean. Germany announced in 1917 that it would freely sink ships without warning in the Atlantic. This put both military and civilian ships at risk. Repeated attacks helped convince the United States to join the war.

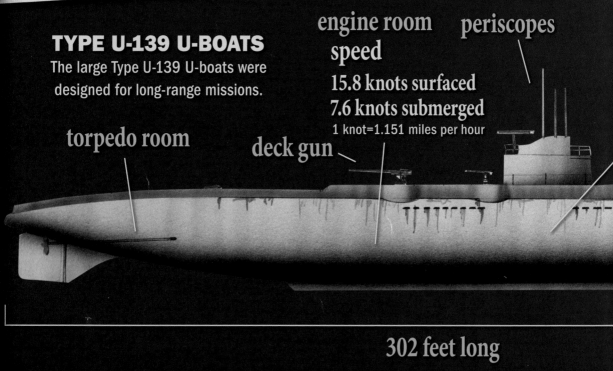

TYPE U-139 U-BOATS
The large Type U-139 U-boats were designed for long-range missions.

engine room

periscopes

speed
15.8 knots surfaced
7.6 knots submerged
1 knot=1.151 miles per hour

torpedo room

deck gun

302 feet long

U-35
the name of the U-boat that sank the most enemy ships during World War I

194
ships sunk by *U-35* while under the command of Captain Lothar von Arnauld de la Perière

453,000 tons
combined weight of the ships sunk by *U-35*

A torpedo from a U-boat hits a ship.

10 million Allied tonnage, including ships and supplies, sunk by U-boats

334 German U-boats built by the end of the war

430 Allied ships sunk by U-boats in April 1917 alone

6 German U-boats at sea at any given time

control room

crew quarters
62 crew carried

torpedo room
24 torpedoes carried

deck gun

37 feet high

tonnage—the weight of ships and the cargo they carry, measured in tons

Spying in World War I

Room 40 name of the British Naval Intelligence organization that decoded and intercepted German messages during the war

June 15, 1917 date the United States established the **Espionage** Act, a law making it a crime for U.S. citizens to spy for or aid enemy nations

Allied soldiers search a suspected spy.

espionage—spying

235 Allied spies convicted of espionage by the Germans

11 German spies executed for espionage at the Tower of London during World War I

Tower of London

Animal Spies

100,000 approximate number of carrier pigeons used by the Germans and the British to carry secret messages

95 percentage of messages carrier pigeons successfully delivered

12 important messages delivered by the Allied carrier pigeon Cher Ami

1 dog and 2 cats animals suspected of spying on British troops for the German military. They were seen crossing into British trenches, where British soldiers thought they may have been carrying secret messages.

Weapons

Rifles

200 yards approximate range of the M1917 Enfield rifle

46.3 inches length of the Enfield rifle

1,123,259 Enfields sent to France for U.S. use by 1918

6 rounds the Enfield's magazine could hold

75 percentage of AEF soldiers who were armed with the M1917 Enfield by the end of the war

howitzer—a short cannon that shoots shells in a high arc
casualty—a soldier who is dead, wounded, missing, or captured after a battle

Hand Grenades

250,000 average number of hand grenades the British produced every week during the war

7 seconds time after activation that U.S. and British hand grenades exploded

5.5 seconds time after activation that German hand grenades exploded

Artillery

420 millimeters diameter of the ammunition used in the German **howitzer** nicknamed "Big Bertha." (That is as big around as a large pizza.)

70% estimated battle **casualties** caused by artillery during the war

BIG BERTHA

1,807 pounds weight of the shells Big Bertha fired

Battle of

The AEF fought German forces in the summer of 1918 in a forest in northeastern France known as Belleau Wood. It was the first large battle fought by U.S. forces and the first where they suffered heavy casualties. Despite huge losses, the AEF fought back the Germans and took the woods for the Allies.

June 1: U.S. troops dig a defensive line.

June 2: German troops reach Belleau Wood.

June 4: U.S. troops defeat a major German assault.

June 6: U.S. troops launch two assaults, including one on Hill 142. They suffer more than 1,000 casualties during the attacks.

Belleau Wood

U.S. Casualties

1,811 killed

7,996 wounded

200
Allied ambulances needed to carry the wounded on June 23 alone

14 hours
time the June 25 Allied artillery bombardment lasted, allowing U.S. forces to capture the forest and clear out German troops

June 11: After an artillery attack, U.S. troops move forward, capturing two-thirds of Belleau Wood.

June 25: Allied troops use artillery and machine guns to clear remaining German forces from Belleau Wood.

June 13: The German forces launch a counterattack, which includes the use of poison gas.

June 26: U.S. troops defeat German counterattacks and take control of Belleau Wood.

Disease and World War I

Influenza

In 1918 a severe strain of the influenza virus spread across the globe. Nicknamed the Spanish Flu, the deadly strain killed civilians and soldiers alike.

1918

March 11
U.S. Army private reports to the camp hospital at Fort Riley in Kansas with flu symptoms.

July 22
Philadelphia public health officials issue the first public bulletin about the flu.

August 27
U.S. Navy sailors in Boston, Massachusetts, report flu symptoms.

October 6
Philadelphia reports 289 deaths from flu in a single day.

Trench Foot

Trench foot occurs when feet stay wet for long periods of time. Trenches were often damp, and many had inches of standing water. Trench foot caused pain, swelling, and blisters. In severe cases, when blisters dried, the affected skin and tissue fell off a soldier's foot.

2,000 American injuries attributed to trench foot

75,000 British injuries attributed to trench foot

3 pairs of socks each British soldier was required to have to help keep his feet dry

25–50 million
approximate number of total worldwide deaths caused by influenza in 1918–1919

340,000
U.S. soldiers hospitalized for influenza in 1918

227,000
U.S. soldiers hospitalized for battle wounds in 1918

October 22
New York City reports 869 deaths from flu in a single day.

December 4
U.S. War Department reports 20,000 soldiers have died from the flu.

Shell Shock

Soldiers in World War I experienced devastating casualties, terrifying weapons, and harsh living conditions. The realities of service caused some soldiers to acquire a mental health condition called shell shock. Symptoms varied, but many with the condition experienced anxiety, hallucinations, nightmares, and loss of appetite.

1917
year a British doctor introduced the term "shell shock"

80,000 British cases of shell shock by the end of the war

4/5 proportion of British shell shock sufferers who were unable to return to military duty

hallucination—seeing something that looks and seems real but is not real

World War I by the 11s

M1911
code for U.S. Army uniform

11 million
approximate number of German troops who fought in World War I

11:30 a.m.
time of day Archduke Franz Ferdinand died, putting the war in motion

11th-Month Events

First Battle of Ypres ends **(11/22/1914)**

Battle of the Somme ends **(11/18/1916)**

Russian Tsar Nicholas II is overthrown and Vladimir Lenin takes power **(11/7/1917)**

Month, day, and time when Germany surrenders to the Allies

11TH month day hour

(11:00 a.m. on November 11, 1918)

Aftermath

total number of wounded in World War I, all sides	21,189,154
total number killed in World War I, all sides	8,528,831

5 million   10 million   15 million   20 million

57.5%
soldiers on all sides who became casualties in World War I

42.5%
soldiers who did not become casualties

6,000
number of soldiers on all sides who died every day of the war on average

6.6 million
number of civilian deaths on all sides in World War I

200,000

204,002
total number of U.S. soldiers wounded

150,000

116,516
total number of U.S. soldiers killed

100,000

50,000

1.5 billion

estimated number of shells fired on the western front during World War I

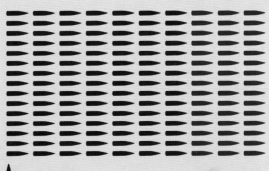

30

percentage of those shells that never exploded, some of which are still in the ground

= 10 million shells

4,355,000

total number of U.S. soldiers who served during World War I

14

number of points in U.S. President Woodrow Wilson's plan for peace in Europe after the war. They included freedom of travel on the seas and the creation of an international group to handle future disputes.

GLOSSARY

alliance (uh-LYE-uns)—an agreement to join together

assassination (uh-sas-eh-NAY-shun)—a murder of a government official or other leader

casualty (KAZH-yuhl-tee)—a soldier who is dead, wounded, missing, or captured after a battle

espionage (ES-pee-uh-nahzh)—spying

expeditionary (ek-spuh-DISH-uh-nayr-ee)—sent on military service in a different country

front (FRUNT)—the area where two opposing armies meet and fight

hallucination (huh-loo-suh-NAY-shun)—seeing something that looks and seems real but is not real

howitzer (HOU-uht-sur)—a short cannon that shoots shells in a high arc

mobilize (MO-buh-lyz)—to make ready for war

province (PROV-ins)—a division of a country, similar to a state

range (RAYNJ)—the longest distance at which a weapon can still hit its target

telegram (TEL-uh-gram)—a message transmitted over a long distance

tonnage (TUN-ij)—the weight of ships and the cargo they carry, measured in tons

READ MORE

Adams, Simon. *World War I.* Eyewitness. New York: DK Publishing, 2014.

Cooke, Tim. *World War I on the Front Lines.* Life on the Front Lines. North Mankato, Minn.: Capstone Press, 2014.

Kenney, Karen Latchana. *Everything World War I.* Everything Series. Washington, D.C.: National Geographic Society, 2014.

CRITICAL THINKING USING THE COMMON CORE

1. Many deadly weapons were used during World War I. Of all the weapons, which type caused the most casualties? (Key Ideas and Details)

2. How does the timeline on pages 24 and 25 help you understand the impact of influenza on the war? How did the effects of influenza compare with battle injuries? Support your answer with at least two other online or print sources. (Integration of Knowledge and Ideas)

INTERNET SITES

FactHound offers a safe, fun way to find Internet sites related to this book. All of the sites on FactHound have been researched by our staff.

Visit *www.facthound.com*

Type in this code: 9781491442968

INDEX

TITLES IN THIS SET:

The American **Revolution** BY THE **NUMBERS**

THE **CIVIL WAR** BY THE **NUMBERS**

WORLD **WAR I** BY THE **NUMBERS**

WORLD **WAR II** BY THE **NUMBERS**